The Battles of
the *Constitution*

The Battles of
the *Constitution*

Old Ironsides and the Freedom of the Seas

by Robert Goldston

The Macmillan Company
Collier-Macmillan Ltd., London

The Macmillan Company
Collier-Macmillan Canada, Ltd., Toronto, Ontario

Library of Congress catalog card number: 71-78084
Printed in the United States of America
FIRST PRINTING

PICTURE CREDITS: Franklin D. Roosevelt Library, 15, 16, 20-21, 30-31, 59, 63, 66–67, 74, 80; Historical Pictures Service–Chicago, 5, 12, 33, 40, 43, 45, 46, 50, 54, 56, 61, 72, 77; U.S. Naval Academy Museum, title page, 6–7, 22, 23, 26, 28, 36–37, 38, 49 (left), 49 (right), 76, 82. Picture research by Patricia Crum.

COVER ILLUSTRATION, Historical Pictures Service–Chicago

For William Karakas II

Contents

1

Birth of a Frigate,
Birth of a Navy

September 20, 1797. by 10 a.m. captain isaiah shaw, and for that matter, the entire crew of the U.S. merchant ship *Argosy* knew their luck had run out. The light, baffling winds of the Mediterranean, shifting fitfully from quarter to quarter, were driving them slowly but steadily toward the North African coast. Their pursuers, two light-draft, lateen-rigged ketches, designed especially for cruising in these waters and commanded by captains who were, no doubt, intimately familiar with the shoals of this region, were steadily gaining. And now, off the port bow, another lateen-rigged ship, a brig, was bearing down on them. Within an hour on her present course *Argosy* must fetch up on a shoal.

Even if the wind should shift she lacked the speed to out-distance her enemies. Captain Shaw was faced with an un-pleasant decision.

The ketches and the brig flew the crescent and star flag of the Bey (the ruler) of Algiers (not that Captain Shaw needed to see it—he could tell the cut of an Algerian cruiser without reference to flags), and through his telescope Shaw could see their decks crammed with ragged but fierce-look-ing ruffians armed to the teeth with pistols, cutlasses and daggers. Although the ketches carried only four small cannon each and the brig eight, that was exactly sixteen more cannon than *Argosy* mounted. While Algerian gunnery was not noticeably accurate, the cruisers needed but a few hits to cripple the thin-sided American Baltimore clipper. And if it came to a fight and the Algerians carried *Argosy* by board-ing, they might, in their excitement, kill every man-jack of the crew; such cases were not unknown.

Of course the Algerians would much prefer to take *Argosy* without a fight. Then her cargo (Italian glass and silk) would enrich the coffers of the Bey, the ship would join the Algerian merchant fleet and the crew—well, both Captain Shaw and his crew would naturally be enslaved. They would have heavy iron shackles locked onto their feet and be thrown into the slave pens of Algiers, there to work in the stone quarries, eat vinegar and bread once a day and rot until death, God or the United States government came to their aid—the last named by paying a heavy ransom.

Captain Shaw folded his telescope, glanced once at the silent, intent faces of his crew staring up at him from the deck where they'd assembled like sheep waiting in a butcher's pen, turned to his first mate and said quietly, "Strike the flag, Mr. Williams, bring her into the wind and drop sails."

As his orders were hastily obeyed, the captain looked away to the horizon. Not that he was looking for help. There were no United States warships to protect American commerce in the Mediterranean (or anywhere else for that matter)—there was no United States navy. And filling Captain Shaw's cup of bitterness to the brim was the knowledge that no state of war existed between Algiers and the United States. After all, why should the powerful Bey of Algiers bother to declare war on such a despicably powerless nation? Now, over the water, Captain Shaw could hear cheers rising from the decks of the Algerian cruisers as *Argosy*'s flag fluttered down and her bow came into the wind. . . .

It would not have comforted Captain Shaw to know that his was not the only luck to run out that day. Half a world away, after a six-hour chase, the U.S. merchantman *Salem* of Boston, Captain Richard Weaver commanding, had fallen prey to the French frigate *Insurgente* just ten miles off the coast of the Caribbean island of Santo Domingo. The big French frigate (she mounted 40 guns) was one of the fastest warships afloat. Yet clipper-rigged *Salem* had led her a merry chase, might never have been captured at all had it not been for a lucky shot from one of *Insurgente*'s bow-chasers that carried away *Salem*'s wheel and made a bloody mash of her helmsman.

Now Captain Weaver was listening to a young French lieutenant, very elegant in his gaudy uniform, jabber rapidly at him in broken English. *Salem* was a smuggler of course? No, Weaver replied hopelessly, she was an American ship lawfully engaged in trade, carrying rum and textiles, bound for Antigua, another island in the Caribbean. But, protested the lieutenant, was Captain Weaver not aware that Antigua was now a British possession, and was he not aware that

Great Britain was the eternal enemy of the French Republic and was he not therefore aware that the *Salem*'s cargo was contraband? No, Captain Weaver was aware of no such sea law—but was the captain of *Insurgente* himself not aware that his frigate was engaged in simple piracy? The French lieutenant shrugged and turned away. His prize crew were even now scrambling up *Salem*'s rigging, preparing to set sail while several of *Insurgente*'s carpenters were rigging up a complicated jury of ropes to replace the smashed wheel.

Like Captain Shaw in the distant Mediterranean, Captain Weaver knew that argument was useless. He knew that his cargo was forfeit and his ship would be taken into the nearest French port to be auctioned off before a prize-court. He and his men would be turned loose to rot or starve on the nearest Caribbean beach. Weaver knew his argument to be useless because there was no American navy to give point to it. In fact there was no state of war in existence between France and the United States. Why should the conquering French Republic bother to declare war on a collection of backwoods farmers it considered too parsimonious or, more likely, too lily-livered to protect themselves on the high seas? In the French lieutenant's shrug, in the studied insolence of his be-havior, in the blood-stained deck beneath him, Captain Weaver read an old and primal law of the sea: the strong take what they will, the weak suffer what they must.

But the boarding of *Argosy* by Algerians and the capture of *Salem* by the French navy were not the only notable events of September 20, 1797. For on the same day, far to the north in Massachusetts, while a crisp autumn wind made scores of flags snap and a fife-and-drum corps tootled merrily amid the cheers of shipwrights, seamen and thousands of onlookers, the United States frigate *Constitution* slid down

Launching of the frigate Constitution *in 1797*

A view of Boston harbor in the late 1700's

the greased ways of Colonel Claghorn's shipyard into the cold waters of Boston harbor. She was long and graceful; even without her spars and rigging she showed promise of speed. And she was sturdy; even without cannon poking from her rows of gunports she looked powerful. In fact only the *Constitution*'s designers and builders suspected the truth —that pound for pound she was the most powerful warship ever built. As the Bey of Algiers and the new French Republic would soon learn to their sorrow, the despicable nation of backwoods farmers was about to flex its muscles on the high seas.

"Millions for defense, but not one cent for tribute!"

Yet tribute, both direct and indirect, was exactly what Americans had been paying ever since the Revolution. Why? For several reasons. For one, England and the revolutionary French Republic had gone to war—that long and desperate struggle which was to develop into the Napoleonic Wars and torture Europe for a generation. Every nation in the Old World was to become involved, and their ships therefore became lawful prize to cruisers of one side or the other. But the United States remained neutral. American farmers were now producing a surplus of food that the warring powers of Europe desperately needed—and what with the English blockade of the continent and French cruisers sweeping the seas, this food could be carried only in American ships. While colonial American sea-borne trade had always been important (75 per cent of all British trade had been carried in American-built ships before 1776), now it reached global proportions. The American merchant marine

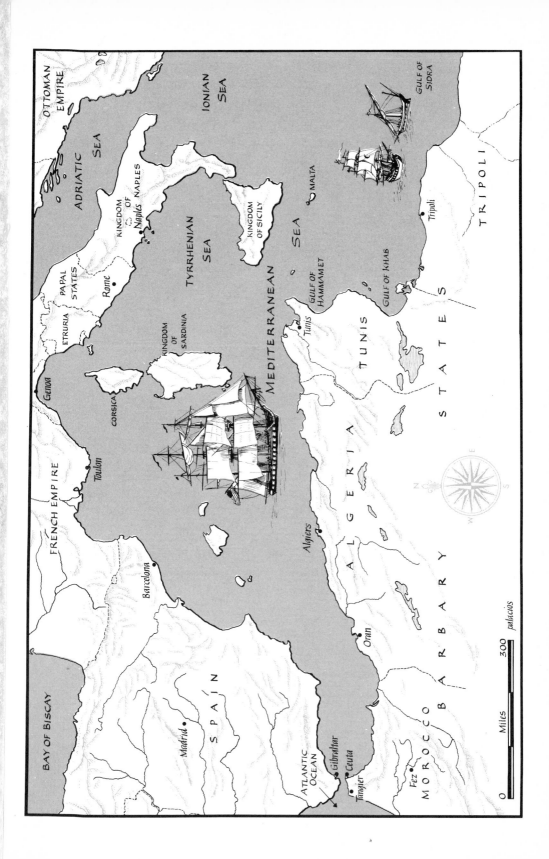

was second only to the English in size. Since the French fleet was too weak to combat the English blockade directly or to impose its own blockade of the British Isles, the burgeoning American merchant-marine trade with England could be attacked only through privateering (legalized piracy) backed up by the power of individual French warships. Whether such undeclared warfare was legitimate or not, American commerce was tempting prey to the French. It was tempting too to the Barbary pirates.

Who were the Barbary pirates? The decayed remnants of the once mighty Moslem empire; the four North African states of Algiers, Morocco, Tunis and Tripoli which had lived by Mediterranean piracy for hundreds of years. Small nations such as Denmark, Portugal, Naples and the United States paid the states tribute to leave their commerce alone. Great nations such as England or France paid them subsidies to enable them to keep on preying on neutral vessels, thereby imposing on neutral merchant marines the same losses suffered by their own through the wars.

When one of the Beys or Deys of the Barbary states decided he needed gold or slaves or diversion, he declared war on one of the smaller nations by chopping down its flagpole in front of its consulate and throwing the unfortunate consul into a dungeon. Then he sent forth his swarms of small but deadly Mediterranean cruisers to take that nation's ships. The crews were enslaved, the cargoes sold and the ships added to the Bey's own fleet. Christian slaves could later be ransomed at a stiff price if they survived long enough. And peace could be had by negotiating a new treaty with the Bey and paying him a handsome tribute. The entire system today would be called a "protection racket."

In 1792 the newly assembled United States Senate had

authorized a payment of $100,000 annually to Algiers, Tunis and Tripoli plus an additional $40,000 ransom for American crews then held in slavery. Despite this munificent bribe, the very next year (1793) eleven American merchantmen were taken by the Algerians and their "infidel" crews enslaved. This caused President George Washington to appeal to Congress for funds to build a navy to deal with these gangsters. But Congress was economy-minded and a navy would cost a lot of tax money. Furthermore, many Congressmen, thinking no doubt of the English naval-officer aristocracy, considered a navy a threat to Republican institutions. Besides, England ruled the seas—a navy might somehow get the new nation into conflict with Britain.

So while Congress grudgingly authorized the building of six frigates in 1794, it specified strictly that if peace should be made with Algiers construction work on the warships must stop. Peace was in fact made with Algiers in 1795 and the half-completed frigates were held on their ways in Philadelphia, New York, Boston and Baltimore. The total cost of the six frigates would reach $700,000; the cost of the new treaty with Algiers was more than $1,000,000 plus a 36-gun ship (a "gift" to the Bey personally) to help the Algerians carry on their piracy in the future. Nevertheless Congress congratulated itself on having saved money.

On the ways the nascent American navy rested still-born until 1797. By that time it was the French who were wrecking American commerce as part of their war against England. It was estimated that, aside from regular French naval vessels, there were more than 150 French privateers (privately owned and manned ships authorized by a government to make war on enemy commerce) operating in the Caribbean alone. This was bringing the vital American-West Indian trade to

An American captain delivers tribute money to the Bey of Algiers

a standstill. A group of New England sea captains sent a petition for action to the Secretary of State listing twenty-seven American merchant vessels seized by the French—and that was but a fraction of the total.

John Adams had become President in 1797 and he sent three commissioners to negotiate a settlement of the problem with the French government. But that government was now the "Directory," the last, least revolutionary and most corrupt of the pre-Napoleonic French governments. Its members boldly demanded both official and personal bribes—totaling something close to $50,000,000 in today's currency. It was then that Commissioner Charles C. Pinckney banged his fist down on the negotiating table and cried: "Millions for defense, but not one cent for tribute!" The news of Pinckney's defiance thrilled the United States, and while citizens marched through the streets wearing Adams' black cockades in their hats and bands blared the new patriotic song "Hail Columbia," the United States navy was suddenly and unexpectedly born.

*"We are to consider what ships will be
most formidable . . ."*

Those six frigates waiting completion since 1794 were going to be formidable indeed. When Washington first received congressional approval for their construction, he had commissioned Philadelphia Quaker Joshua Humphreys, a junior partner in the marine-designing firm of Wharton & Humphreys, to work out a basic design for the new frigates. Humphreys was the greatest naval architect of his day, perhaps of any day.

"As our navy will for a considerable time be inferior in numbers," he wrote to Washington, "we are to consider what size ships will be most formidable and be an overmatch for those of the enemy; such frigates as in blowing weather would be an overmatch for double-deck ships and in light winds to evade coming into action. Frigates will be the first object, and none ought to be built less than 150 foot keel, to carry thirty 24-pounders on the gundeck. Ships of this construction have everything in their favor, their great length gives them an advantage of sailing, which is an object of the first magnitude."

These were grandiose conceptions indeed. The normal French or English frigate of that day was about 125 feet long and carried a total of thirty-six 18-pound cannon (that is, guns which threw an 18-pound cannonball). The 24-pounder was exclusively a line-of-battleship gun, much too heavy for the weaker timbers of a frigate—putting 24-pounders aboard frigates would make the ships clumsy and unmaneuverable. But Humphreys solved the structural problem by using enormous beams and bracing. Yet wouldn't this extra weight make the ships too slow? No, because Humphreys gave them the lines of the sleek Baltimore clippers. This plus their greater length and the tremendous sweep of their masts (more than 200 feet from the deck) would give them the necessary speed to run from line-of-battleships, dance around opposing frigates and even run down swift sloops and corvettes.

The new frigates slid down the ways in 1797—first *United States,* 44 (a ship's classification was determined by the number of guns she carried, which number always followed her name; thus the frigate *United States* carried 44 guns), followed by *Constellation,* 38, *Constitution,* 44, *President,* 44, *Congress,* 38, and *Chesapeake,* 38. Every one of these ships was to make a great name for itself, yet through the slight differences in her building, the luck of her captains and the devotion of her crews, *Constitution* alone was to achieve immortality in that historical pantheon of ships such as Drake's *Golden Hind,* Worden's *Monitor* and Nelson's *Victory* preserved in historical imagination.

Constitution *rigged for battle*

In 1797, all that was hidden in the future. The new frigates excited only general derision from such experts as British naval officers. Yet look at *Constitution* closely. She was three-masted (Colonel Claghorn's workmen had, for good luck, placed a golden coin under the heel of her foremast, a silver coin under the mainmast and a copper coin under the mizzenmast while she was still on the ways) and square-rigged (that is, her sails were rectangular, carried from yards that ran across her masts), able to set seventy-two sails with a total of 43,000 square feet of canvas. Her mainmast was more than 233 feet tall, her mizzenmast over 180 feet. She had an overall length of 204 feet and a water-line length of 175 feet. Her beam (widest measurement of width) was more than 43 feet and her draft (depth below water) was 22 feet. Her tonnage (figured as the amount of water she displaced, not the amount of freight she could carry) was about 2,000 tons. She was built of live oak and red cedar and her sides supported an "armor" of oak about 22 inches thick. Below her water line she had copper sheathing to fight barnacles, the sheathing coming from the copper and silver works of Paul Revere of Boston. Yet for all her bulk and weight she could *average* 13 knots speed (a knot is a nautical mile, slightly longer than a land mile).

Although *Constitution* was rated a 44-gun ship, she often carried more. On her main deck were the big batteries of 24-pounders, on her upper spar deck lighter guns. The 24-pounders were heavy cast-iron cannon ten feet long mounted on wooden carriages, their blunt snouts protruding through gun ports cut into *Constitution*'s sides. They were loaded from the muzzle—first a wad of gunpowder, then the cannonball, both rammed home by a long-handled rammer.

"Old Ironsides" boasted 44 guns (from a photograph taken in the early 1900's)

The gunpowder was ignited at a small hole (the touchhole) at the rear of the gun by means of a slow-burning "match" or sometimes a spark from a flintlock. After the gun had fired, it was hauled back on its carriage by means of ropes, turned, swabbed out with a long-handled sponge and re-loaded. Heavy work, requiring a tough and well-muscled gun crew for each cannon.

To get these crews President Adams would have to lure them away from the high-paying and relatively easier life of the American merchant marine. The French might draft their crews, the British might "impress" theirs (that is, simply kidnap them from the streets, fields and prisons); the Americans would have to convince theirs that the navy was an attractive proposition. So Adams offered a very appealing rate of pay. Wages were set at $15 to $17 per month plus found (room and board), which was an average of $7 per month more than merchant ships paid and higher than the prevailing rate for mechanics ashore. In addition it was decreed that there would be prize money for all (that is, a share of the proceeds from the sale of captured vessels and cargoes) at a fixed rate per ton and gun of the captures—with double prize money if the enemy was of superior force. Sailors were invited to take a look at the roomy quarters in the big new frigates and to cast an eye over a ration bill set so high that American sailors would get more to eat in two days than the British did in a week. It looked something like this:

> *Sunday:* One and one-half pounds of beef and one-half pound of rice.
> *Monday:* One pound of pork, one-half pint of peas and one-half pound of rice.

> *Tuesday:* One and one-half pounds of beef and one pound
>   of potatoes.
> *Wednesday:* One-half pound of rice, two ounces of butter
>   and six ounces of molasses.
> *Thursday:* One pound of pork and one-half pint of peas.
> *Friday:* One pound of salt fish, one pound of potatoes and
>   two ounces of butter.
> *Saturday:* One pound of pork, one-half pint of peas and
>   four ounces of cheese.
> *Every day:* One-half pint of rum or one quart of beer.

The meat might be salted in casks and wormy, the bread
might be baked rock-hard and wonderfully weevily—but
this was the richest bill of fare ever seen in any nation's navy.
In any event, between the high pay, the roomy quarters, the
rich food and many an American sailor's private vendetta
against the Barbary or French pirates, the new navy rapidly
filled up with tough, experienced seamen; the same men
who'd been sailing their Baltimore clippers from Shanghai
to Bristol and all the world's ports in between.

To officer his new navy Adams had a wealth of experienced merchant captains and privateersmen to draw upon.
To attract the best, he again set high wages; a captain drew
$75 per month plus six rations a day figured at twenty-eight
cents each; a lieutenant made $50 plus three rations, warrant
officers $20 and two rations. But well as these captains knew
the sea and the wind, personally brave as they might be,
they were not true naval officers operating within an estab-
lished naval tradition. As the new frigates put to sea, the
atmosphere aboard each of them was different, depending on
the whim of the captain. Some, like Thomas Truxtun's
Constellation, were run taut; that is, with strict discipline
and daily gunnery practice. Others, like John Barry's *United*

States, had the lax discipline of merchant ships. Some captains were simply incompetent, unable to fit themselves into the demands of a naval service.

Among the incompetents was Captain Samuel Nicholson, first commander of *Constitution*, a Maryland merchant captain who owed his appointment to political pull. When the new frigate first put to sea on July 4, 1798, Captain Nicholson felt so uncertain about his new command that direction of the ship was left largely to the lieutenants. Nicholson had orders to cruise down the Atlantic seaboard from Cape Henry, Virginia, to Florida and search out French privateers. Although the seas were swarming with them, Captain Nicholson managed not to spot a single one. When *Constitution* returned to Boston for refitting after her cruise, Nicholson was relieved and command of the ship given to Silas Talbot, an ex-army officer who had been a successful privateersman during the Revolution.

Perhaps it wasn't Nicholson's fault after all. For Talbot was as aggressive as any captain in the new navy, yet the most exciting action *Constitution* saw under his command was the handy winning of a race against a new English frigate in the West Indies. For the rest it was a matter of constant patrol among the Caribbean islands—and of sharp, fierce engagements between *Constitution*'s attendant squadron of light-draft sloops and schooners and the small French privateers who hugged the coasts and inlets in waters too shallow for the big frigate to enter. Although *Constitution* was not to fire a single shot in anger during the undeclared war against France, her presence, and that of the other new frigates supporting the lighter vessels, had a notable effect; insurance rates on American merchantmen in Caribbean waters dropped by $8,500,000—a saving which was almost

*Construction of
a frigate at
Joshua Humphreys'
Philadelphia shipyards*

four times the cost of the entire American navy.

And *Constitution*'s officers and men were learning their trade too. They learned it on some of the smaller vessels, like *Experiment*, 12, a schooner that beat off more than a dozen heavily armed pirate barges, killing hundreds of their crew in a four-hour battle off the coast of Haiti. Or like *Enterprise*, 12, a clipper that took more than eighteen heavily armed French privateers with a total of 42 guns, three hundred prisoners and killed about sixty of the enemy in various actions—which was quite a record for a ship of but 12 guns and seventy crewmen.

They learned by example too and by the talk and bragging and gossip at shoreside taverns where sailors gathered and compared notes. Especially the sailors talked of Thomas Truxtun and *Constellation*; about how the old man had fired all his junior officers but one (a lad named David Porter) after the first cruise; how he had issued detailed letters of instruction to each of his officers on how they must do their jobs; how he drilled his men at the great guns hour after

Captain Thomas Truxtun

Constellation *opens fire on* L'Insurgente

hour; how he took *Constellation* into action against *Insurgente* (Captain Weaver would have rejoiced) and reduced that French frigate to a flaming wreck in less than an hour; and, finally, how he pitted *Constellation*'s 38 guns against the 50 guns of the French frigate *Vengeance* and dismasted her, riddled her hull and killed a third of her crew before the beaten Frenchman (she'd surrendered three times during the fight but nobody noticed through the smoke and flame of battle) escaped under cover of nightfall.

By 1800 the conquering French Republic had had enough of the new American frigates, enough too of their heavily drilled gunners and grim captains. The troubles between the United States and France were settled by a convention signed in Paris (no one talking now of tribute), and the Caribbean, not to mention the entire Atlantic, was safe for American merchantmen. But if the officers and crew of *Constitution* regretted that they had not had a chance to prove themselves and their ship in action, they need not have fretted—their chance was coming sooner than anyone expected.

2

The
Shores of Tripoli

IT WAS IN MAY 1801 THAT THE PASHA OF TRIPOLI SENT OUT his chief axman to chop down the flagpole of the United States consul, thereby declaring war and loosing his Mediterranean cruisers to resume their captures of American merchantmen. Some time later he informed the United States government that peace could be bought for a mere $250,000. The government to which the Pasha addressed himself was now headed by President Thomas Jefferson, and since Mr. Jefferson had declared himself in favor only of a navy for defense, and against foreign wars of all kinds, the Pasha logically expected tribute. In fact Mr. Jefferson had declared, only six months before, "We are running navigation mad, and commerce and Navy mad, which is worst of all." The new President's avowed ideal was that of a democratic nation of farmers, as self-sufficient as possible, defended by small harbor gunboats.

But Mr. Jefferson was a man of many ideas, some of which conflicted. One of them was that payment of tribute or ransom to the Barbary pirates was unworthy of the United States. So when the news came in from Tripoli, Jefferson immediately dispatched a squadron consisting of *President*, 44, *Philadelphia*, 38, the light frigate *Essex*, 32, and the little schooner *Enterprise*, 12, to blockade Tripoli. By July 1801, the ships were cruising in the Mediterranean, using Gibraltar as a base. They convoyed American merchantmen and set up a rather inefficient blockade of Tripoli. *Enterprise* came across a Tripolitan 14-gun brig and shot it to pieces, but that was the only positive result of the campaign of 1801. Nevertheless it was more than was gained by the campaign of 1802, during which the American Mediterranean squadron made so little impact on the Barbary pirates that the Emperor of Morocco copied his Tripolitan friends and declared war on the United States.

Jefferson and his Secretary of the Navy put their heads together and decided that one of the main reasons for the navy's ineffectiveness against the Barbary states was jealousy among the ship's captains and a lack of discipline throughout the squadron. To correct these matters for the forthcoming campaign of 1803, they decided to place a relatively unknown captain in charge of the squadron. This turned out to be Edward Preble, a slightly built, frosty-faced person from Maine who suffered from stomach ulcers and was reputed to have a violent temper. He had served as a lieutenant aboard a Massachusetts state ship during the Revolution and

Captain Edward Preble

during the troubles with France he had commanded *Essex* on Caribbean convoy duty and, later, a long cruise to the East Indies. So he had had little chance to arouse the jealousy of other captains who barely knew him. In fact, when he was shown the list of captains and lieutenants who would be serving under his command, and found that they averaged twenty years younger than himself, he roared, "Nothing but a pack of boys!"—a phrase that was to become famous later. Along with his "pack of boys," the government gave him *Constitution* as his flagship, *Philadelphia*, 38, *Argus* and *Siren* of 16 guns each, and *Vixen*, *Nautilus* and *Enterprise* of 12 guns each.

When Preble stepped aboard his flagship, *Constitution*, he declared to the assembled officers and crew, "The honor of the American flag is very dear to me, and I hope it will not be tarnished under my command." By which, the men of the new Mediterranean squadron soon learned, Preble meant he hoped none of *them* would dare to tarnish it under his command. And he ran a taut ship and a taut squadron—even tauter than Truxtun had run *Constellation*. Notes and signals indicating the Commodore's displeasure over one matter or another flew from *Constitution* to the other ships like broadsides. The younger officers and the crews grumbled mightily about it all, muttering about "such tyranny," until they found out what Preble was made of. The men aboard *Constitution* found out during their voyage to the Mediterranean.

It was on a pitch-black night approaching Gibraltar that a heavy ship loomed up alongside *Constitution* and the two ships hailed each other demanding to learn the other's identity without disclosing their own. Preble grew irritated. "I now hail for the last time," he shouted. "If you do not answer I'll fire a shot."

"If you do, I'll answer with a broadside," replied the captain of the strange vessel.

"I should like to see you try that!" Preble bellowed. "I now hail for an answer; what ship is that?"

"This is His Britannic Majesty's ship *Donegal*, 84, Sir Richard Strachan. Send a boat aboard."

"This is the United States frigate *Constitution*, 44, Captain Edward Preble, and I'll be damned if I'll send a boat aboard any ship. Blow up your matches, boys!"

The Englishman turned out not to be a line-of-battleship after all, only a 32-gun frigate, and *they* sent the boat. But that wasn't the point. The point, which spread through the squadron like fire, was that grim old Preble was fully prepared to take *Constitution* into action against a foe presumably twice her size. There was steel in the man.

The Emperor of Morocco found this out also. When the American squadron assembled at Gibraltar, Preble dispatched *Philadelphia* to blockade Tripoli, while he took *Constitution* and the smaller ships to look into Tangier, the Moroccan capital. It was a risky business. The port of Tangier was a

Constitution *under full sail*

wide crescent, and every part of it was commanded by heavy cannon set behind thick stone parapets. Ships were supposed to have but little chance against heavy shore fortifications in any case, but at Tangier Preble would be vastly outnumbered in guns. Nevertheless he coolly sailed into the middle of the harbor, his squadron's decks cleared for action, every cannon double-shotted, and *Constitution*'s port broadside battery aimed carefully at the Emperor's palace. Thinking matters over, the Emperor decided to grant Preble an interview.

Before he left *Constitution* (accompanied by only two midshipmen) Preble told his officers, "Comrades, the result of the coming interview is known only to God. Be it what it may, during my absence, keep the ships cleared for action. Let every officer and seaman be at his quarters, and if the least injury is offered to any person, immediately attack the batteries, the castle, the city and the troops, totally regardless of me and my personal safety."

When Preble and his two midshipmen approached the Emperor in the great reception hall of the imperial palace, they were told to kneel as was customary.

"Americans do not kneel to any man," Preble declared.

"Are you not afraid you will be detained?" the Emperor demanded.

"No, sir," Preble replied drily. "You do not dare to detain me. But if you should presume to do so, my squadron would lay your batteries, your castle and your city in ruins within one hour."

The Emperor thought that over. From his window he could see the grim warships assembled in the harbor. Finally he declared that he had never intended to make war upon the United States; it must have been some insubordinate

underling who committed "errors." Whereupon the U.S.
consul was released, the flagpole replaced and several captured American merchant ships turned over to the Americans. The treaty with the United States was reaffirmed
without payment of tribute. Commodore Preble sailed away
satisfied—and surrounded now by officers and men who
would have sailed with him through the gates of hell itself.

But when the squadron reached Gibraltar it was to learn
of disaster. The frigate *Philadelphia*, under Captain William
Bainbridge, had been captured by the Tripolitans. It was an
accident (Bainbridge was never blamed)—*Philadelphia*
blockading Tripoli, had given chase to a large Tripolitan brig

and run upon an uncharted reef in Tripoli harbor, heeling over so that none of her guns could be brought to bear in her own defense. The Tripolitans swarmed out with armed barges and shot away at *Philadelphia* until Bainbridge surrendered. Then on the next flood tide, the pirates floated *Philadelphia* off her reef and towed her into port for refitting as part of the Tripolitan navy. Bainbridge, his officers and men were now in the Tripolitan slave pens and, worst of all, while Preble's force was diminished by one fifth, the Pasha's navy had acquired a dangerous warship.

Preble's solution to this problem was to sail directly to Tripoli and impose the tightest blockade on that port it had

The furious Tripolitan attack on the frigate Philadelphia

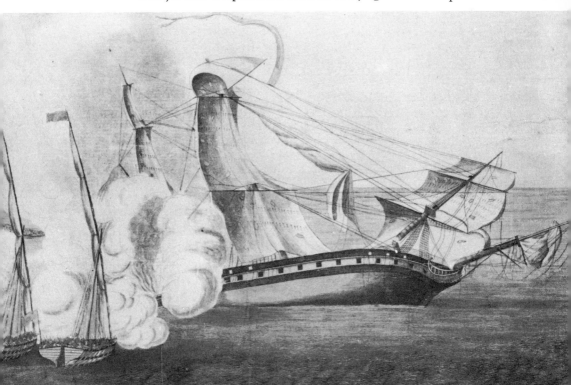

ever seen. It was a savage winter during 1803–1804; there was ice in Venice that year, and Mediterranean storms blew so violently that for weeks the U.S. flag was the only one at sea. But it stayed at sea through the worst weather, and Commodore Preble stayed with it, shifting his quarters from *Constitution* to the other smaller ships in turn to make sure he shared every discomfort with his men. And the corn supplies upon which Tripoli depended for food were completely cut off for the winter. But what about *Philadelphia*, now fitting out as a Tripolitan cruiser?

Preble had an answer to that problem too. He proposed to sail a captured Tripolitan ketch (lateen-rigged so the pirates could not tell it was an enemy) right into Tripoli harbor at night, board *Philadelphia* and blow her up. By this time, so proud were Preble's "boys" of their Commodore and themselves that they fought for the honor of commanding this suicidal mission. Finally, young Stephen Decatur, the lieutenant commanding *Enterprise*, won the job—and every man-jack aboard both *Enterprise* and *Constitution* volunteered to go with him. Decatur selected eighty-four men and began rehearsing them for their desperate task.

The Tripolitan ketch had been renamed, aptly, *Intrepid*, and a Sicilian pilot named Salvator Catalano, who knew Tripoli harbor and could speak Arabic, was enlisted as guide. The plan was to sail into the harbor, board *Philadelphia* and set her afire. No guns would be carried—everything depended on nerve and stealth. On the night of February 16, 1804, under a light breeze and the light of a new moon, *Intrepid* sailed boldly into Tripoli harbor. Most of her eighty-four men were huddled below decks, crowded in with casks of powder and combustibles; the others, dressed in rags, acted the part of a Barbary crew while Catalano stood at the ketch's wheel, jabbering back at the Tripolitans in their own language as *Intrepid* came alongside *Philadelphia*.

At the last moment, just as the two ships touched, the night watch aboard *Philadelphia* caught on and yelled "Americanos!" But it was too late. Within minutes, *Intrepid*'s crew had scrambled up the big frigate's sides and through her gunports with a cheer, driving the surprised Tripolitans overboard or killing them. A few more minutes and the casks of combustibles and explosives had been passed aboard. Rehearsals paid off as *Philadelphia* blazed into a fiery wreck within one quarter of an hour after *Intrepid* touched her. But now the little ketch had to work her way back out of the harbor while dozens of shoreside cannon roared at her. She succeeded and not a man of her crew was so much as scratched. When the great British admiral Lord Horatio Nelson later heard of the deed, he called it "the most bold and daring act of the age."

The Americans were no less impressed with themselves.

Philadelphia *explodes in flames in Tripoli harbor.*

When *Intrepid* returned to the squadron, every ship manned yards and cheered her. Later Congress voted American citizenship for Sicilian Catalano and a full captain's commission for Stephen Decatur. But that fiery young man (he'd been one of those junior officers who'd complained most about Preble's "tyranny") allowed that he was most pleased by a simple, gruff "well done!" from the squadron's commander.

Nor was Preble satisfied yet. He had cut down the odds against him somewhat and troubled the Pasha by his winter blockade. But he wanted to hurt. So as fine weather returned to the Mediterranean, the squadron, led by *Constitution* and reinforced by some Sicilian gunboats armed with a single mortar each, prepared to enter Tripoli harbor to bombard the place.

This bringing of a squadron of wooden warships into a heavily defended harbor was almost as daring an act as Decatur's. Naval doctrine had long held that ships had little chance against stone forts. For one thing, land forts could mount heavier guns than ships; for another, these guns could be protected by yards of stone rather than inches of oak; and, finally, a land fortification could be limitlessly reinforced while ship's crews killed at their guns could not be replaced. Furthermore, Tripoli was generally held to be one of the world's most heavily defended strongholds. Her castles and parapets mounted no less than 115 cannon and the waters of the harbor were defended by twenty armed ships from brigs to barges. As for reinforcements, the Pasha could put 25,000 men behind his guns.

Preble had *Constitution* and a score of little ships, a great contempt for the accuracy of Tripolitan gunnery, confidence in his men and a bold heart. "I expect we shall be hurt

very much," he confided to his log—and went in. The date
was August 3, 1804. With *Constitution* leading the way,
pouring broadsides into the harbor castle so hot and fast that
the Tripolitans were driven from their cannon, the little ships
of the U.S. squadron and the Sicilian gunboats (led by
Decatur) swept into the harbor shooting up everything in
sight.

The fighting lasted about two hours, during which time
the Americans boarded and captured three Tripolitan gunboats in fierce hand-to-hand fighting. What happened to
Decatur himself was typical of the fighting. He had captured one gunboat when word was brought to him that his
brother, James, first lieutenant of the *Nautilus*, had captured
another, only to be killed treacherously by the Tripolitan
captain after he had surrendered. In a fury, Decatur found
that gunboat and with pike in hand led his men to board
her. Finding the captain who had killed his brother, Decatur
went for him with his pike. But the captain was a burly fel-
low and very quick. He got hold of the pike and tried to
turn its needle-sharp point against Decatur. Decatur drew
his cutlass and slashed out only to have it break off at the
hilt, leaving him practically defenseless. He immediately
sprang at the Tripolitan and clutched at his throat with his
bare hands. The two men fell together and rolled on the
deck, the Tripolitan captain trying to draw a dagger, Decatur clutching his throat with one hand while trying to
draw a pistol with the other. He found it finally and pulled
the trigger, firing through his own pocket to kill the Tripolitan.

From that day forth, the Tripolitans, who had been reputed the fiercest hand-to-hand fighters at sea, refused to
engage Americans in close action. But close action was what

August 3, 1804: Commodore Preble's squadron bombards Tripoli.

"Stephen Decatur at Tripoli" (*painting by William A. K. Martin*)

Preble gave them. Almost every day *Constitution*'s big batteries roared away, slowly reducing fortifications and town to rubble, while the smaller ships sank and burned Tripolitan shipping throughout the harbor. And Preble's "boys" came up with a new scheme for hurting the Pasha.

This was as suicidal a mission as Decatur's burning of *Philadelphia*. The idea was to load *Intrepid* with gunpowder, sail her close in under the sea-face of the castle and then blow her up, presumably bringing down the stone walls of the fort through the blast. The crew would escape in two small

boats towed in behind *Intrepid*. Once again Preble was be-
sieged by volunteers. But finally Lieutenant Richard Somers,
commander of the *Nautilus*, was chosen to captain *Intrepid*
and given a dozen volunteers to sail her. Before setting out
on a dark August night, Somers declared that he'd never be
taken alive.

Something went wrong. No one ever knew what, since
there were no survivors. But on the blockading squadron
they saw a tremendous flash of fire and heard the roar of a
gigantic explosion well out in the harbor away from the
castle. Later it was rumored that *Intrepid* had been spotted
and boarded by two Tripolitan cruisers. It was assumed that
Somers had blown himself, his men and his ship up at that
moment.

And still, day by day, every day *Constitution* sailed like a
harbinger of death into Tripoli harbor, smashing up everything in sight. The town was half ruined, soldiers had to be
driven to their guns with whips, the Pasha hid in one of his
deepest dungeons. The French consul brought word that the
Pasha wanted peace—and was prepared to give up his claims
of tribute and ask only a miserable $500 per American ran-
som for his prisoners. The price would undoubtedly have
come down even further, but on September 10, 1804, reinforcements in the form of four more of the big American
frigates reached the Mediterranean. Since all their captains
were senior to Preble, he was superseded as commodore of
the squadron and, taken sick besides, he went home.

As the crusty old captain bid adieu to his "pack of boys"
aboard *Constitution*, Stephen Decatur stepped forward and
presented him with a scroll signed by every officer in the
squadron. Later, Congress would vote him a gold medal and
the thanks of the nation—but the scene aboard *Constitution*

was both a farewell and the recognition of a new beginning. For Preble had created that intangible spirit of pride in service, cool-headed efficiency and boldness of action which gave the new United States navy its basic traditions. All of his officers were to win renown in later battles and to win it in the same spirit of calculated daring that characterized Preble. Ever afterward they called themselves "Preble's boys," and a very good way of getting yourself knocked

An American frigate clashes with an Algerian corsair.

down was to speak disparagingly of the old man in any American seaport.

Preble's departure, however, did not bring peace to the troubled Pasha of Tripoli. Now the accursed American frigates paced back and forth across his harbor mouth in pairs and sailed into town four at a time to blast his city. Stephen Decatur was captain of *Constitution* for seven weeks, then turned her over to captain John Rodgers who kept her (and the rest of the squadron) off Tripoli until June 3, 1805. On that date the Pasha signed a new peace treaty with the United States.

Constitution remained in the Mediterranean for another season—just as a reminder to the Barbary states. It was well she did, for in the autumn of 1806 the Bey of Tunis was heard to threaten the seizure of American merchant ships in the Mediterranean. Rodgers sailed into Tunis harbor and sent a note to the Bey informing him that if he disturbed the peace he "should feel the vengeance of the squadron now in the harbor." The Bey had heard the news from Tripoli. He took a long and careful look at *Constitution*, her decks cleared for action, standing in to his harbor, and decided to keep the peace.

In May 1806 the American squadron was withdrawn from the Mediterranean, its task completed. *Constitution* and one of the brigs pulled into Gibraltar on their way back to Boston. They were watched as they entered the harbor beneath "The Rock" by Admiral Lord Horatio Nelson who was also there with part of Britain's vast Atlantic fleet. His Lordship rubbed his chin thoughtfully and then turned to remark to his aide, "In the handling of those transatlantic ships there is a nucleus of trouble for the Navy of Great Britain." His Lordship was, as usual, right. The trouble was certainly coming—but Nelson could not know how soon.

3

"Hull Her, Boys!"

ONLY SOME PEOPLE WANTED THE WAR—CERTAINLY NOT
the New England merchants and shippers, who contemptu-
ously called it "Mr. Madison's war" and almost took their
states out of the Union rather than fight it. In Congress there
were some Westerners, greedy for new lands and glory
which were presumably to be won in Canada, who called
themselves the "War Hawks." They welcomed the war. But,
overwhelmingly, the War of 1812 was a sailor's war. It was
the American sailor who had the grievance, and because of
this grievance it was he who called into question whether or
not the United States was, in fact, a free and sovereign nation,
even though the Revolution had been fought and won. And

because of this, later historians often refer to the War of 1812 as the second war for independence. In fact the question forcibly brought home to President Madison's administration was, "Did American citizenship mean anything?"

To My Lords of the English Admiralty it meant very little. They were still fighting a world war against Napoleonic France, and the longer that war lasted, the more desperate it became. By at least 1798 it had become almost impossible for the royal navy, Britain's only real weapon against Napoleon, to meet its personnel requirements. Only compulsion could force most Englishmen to take up the harsh and bitter life of sailing in His Majesty's fleets. And

*President
James Madison*

this compulsion took the form of impressment on land (grabbing unwary seamen in ports) and on the sea (stopping merchant vessels and forcibly inducting as many crewmen as His Majesty's captains thought they needed). All of which might not have affected Americans except for the fact that they spoke English, looked English and, often as not, had been born English.

The government of Great Britain did not, at that time, recognize any process by which a born Englishman could become a U.S. citizen. The principle was "Once an Englishman, always an Englishman." And the burden of proof lay upon the unfortunate seaman. Unless he had positive, documentary proof that he had been born in the United States (and what seaman carried such complicated papers?), he was assumed to be English, or at least English enough to fill out the crews of His Majesty's navy. Nor did U.S. State Department protests against impressment of American seamen carry much weight. The usual reply from the admiralty was, "Having no documents to prove his American citizenship, this man is refused to be discharged by their lordships."

By the time Mr. Madison had become President, in 1809, he had personally submitted (as Secretary of State) the cases of more than two thousand American seamen seized from American ships on the high seas and impressed into the royal navy. By 1812 there were more Americans in the royal navy than there were in the United States navy. Nor did British frigates and line-of-battleships prey only on the merchant marine; they did not hesitate to stop and search American men-of-war also.

In 1807 this led to the infamous *Chesapeake* affair. That 38-gun frigate, putting to sea under the command of Captain James Barron (*not* one of Preble's boys), was stopped by

British impressment of U.S. seamen (painting by Howard Pyle)

H.M.S. *Leopard*, 50, off the Virginia capes and ordered to allow a search for deserting British seamen. When *Chesapeake* did not haul to, *Leopard* poured a broadside into her. Aboard *Chesapeake* nothing was ready—the guns were lashed, ammunition stowed below and matches unlit. The only gun the American frigate could fire in reply was touched off by a live coal carried in the bare hands of David Farragut, a midshipman determined to defend the honor of the flag. *Chesapeake* suffered twenty-one casualties, and when the British came aboard they seized four seamen as deserters from the royal navy. It didn't matter that three of the seamen had, in fact, papers and witnesses to prove their American citizenship. Two of them were hanged as an example to others, while the remaining two disappeared into the bowels of British warships. Captain Barron was suspended from the service, and, from that day on, whenever an American warship sailed from harbor it was with guns loaded and ready.

American commerce suffered too. By 1800 the French, for all their imperial decrees about neutrals trading with Britain, could not enforce their rules upon the high seas—they lacked the ships. But the British navy ruled the seas. Not only could it blockade the entire European continent, it even had the

Chesapeake's officers surrender to the British.

ships to spare to station off American ports to examine all incoming and outgoing merchant vessels. My Lords of the Admiralty held that since Britain had proclaimed a blockade of Europe, the mere presence aboard any ship of goods from anywhere in Europe was evidence that the ship had broken the blockade and was, therefore, subject to confiscation. By 1812, then, not only had thousands of American seamen been kidnaped, but hundreds of American merchant vessels had been seized. If New England merchants opposed war with England it was not because they had not been hurt by the English but because they feared they would be hurt more by war.

In 1807 President Thomas Jefferson had tried the old colonial game of boycott against England. No American ships were to put to sea, no American goods to be shipped to England. But the British, it turned out, could stand the loss of trade better than could the Americans. When Mr. Madison became President he lifted the boycott but discovered that "the American found exerted against his national commerce a control indistinguishable in practice from that of colonial days." In the long run, Mr. Madison had to agree with the prophecy of the deceased Benjamin Franklin: "The war of the Revolution has been won, but the war for independence is still to be fought." On June 18, 1812, that struggle, to be called the War of 1812, was declared by Congress.

The Great Race

Of course, in the best American tradition, the United States was utterly unprepared to wage war against anyone in 1812, let alone against the mighty British Empire and its huge royal navy. President Jefferson had decided that since the experience of the Tripolitan wars clearly showed the value of gunboats for coast and harbor defense, and since the United States navy could never hope to be a match for the British, American naval effort should be directed toward the building of gunboats, not frigates. Hundreds of Jefferson's gunboats had been built. They each carried one gun —the recoil of which often swamped the little boats—could not hope to sail on anything stormier than glasslike harbor water, and were often swept ashore by storms.

The "War Hawks" in Congress dreamed of conquering Canada, and, in view of the fact that Great Britain disposed nearly one thousand warships which were acknowledged to be the best in the world, Mr. Madison agreed that the main American war effort would be made on land. To pit the sixteen vessels of the U.S. navy against the British fleet seemed, to the President and his cabinet, madness. So the great Humphreys frigates, the sloops and corvettes built for Mediterranean service, and the miserable gunboats, were assigned the task of harbor defense—were to become nothing more than stationary, floating batteries.

It so happened that two of Preble's boys, Captains William Bainbridge and Charles Stewart, were in Washington when the President reached this decision. They pleaded that the U.S. navy be allowed to sail and fight, if only for the honor of the flag.

"Eight times out of ten," Bainbridge declared, "with equal force we can hardly fail; our men are better men, better disciplined. Our guns are sighted, which is an improvement of our own the English know nothing of. . . . We may be captured and probably shall be, even after taking prizes from them, because their numbers are much greater than ours."

Captain William Bainbridge   *Captain Charles Stewart*

"You will give us victories then, you think?" President Madison demanded impatiently.

"We do," Captain Stewart declared, "and not upon irrational premises."

Madison allowed himself to be convinced. The navy would be allowed to sally forth, its warships making at least one cruise apiece before being laid up for harbor defense.

Commodore John Rodgers, who had been Truxtun's first lieutenant on *Constellation*, immediately sailed out of New York on June 21, 1812, with three of the big frigates and a sloop of war. His objective was the big English Jamaica convoy. He missed the convoy and could not catch a British frigate to which he gave chase. His cruise therefore appeared a failure to Washington. But what Madison's administration failed to realize was that simply by putting to sea with such a powerful force, Rodgers had forced the British to concentrate their warships in American waters—and with the British frigates no longer patrolling the waters off American

*Captain
Isaac Hull*

ports, the far-flung American merchant marine was able to run home with little loss.

Constitution was not part of Rodgers' squadron. War found her in Annapolis, Maryland, under the command of Captain Isaac Hull. This doughty little warrior (he stood barely five feet in his stockings) was from Connecticut. He had sailed against the British in whaleboat expeditions during the Revolution and had been one of the lieutenants who commanded *Constitution* during her first cruise when Captain Nicholson proved incompetent. He had been in charge when *Constitution* won her race against the English frigate in the Caribbean, had seen hot action in sloops and gunboats at

Tripoli and was a charter member of the Preble's Boys Club. When he sailed out of Annapolis on July 12, 1812, he was looking for trouble.

He got more of it than he'd bargained for. On July 17, while sailing about fifteen miles off the New Jersey coast, Hull spotted the sails of a large vessel coming up over the northern horizon. He decided to get closer, hoping she would be an English frigate. She was. But she was the scout of the entire British Halifax squadron, consisting of six big frigates and the line-of-battleship *Belvedere.* Against such overwhelming force Hull had no choice but to run. But at this crucial moment the wind died.

The sea was dead calm, the sails of *Constitution* hung limp and seven British warships stood just beyond gun-shot range. The foremost English frigate, the *Shannon,* fired a few times, but her cannonballs splashed the water short of *Constitution.* Hull bethought himself and put out a kedge; that is, he broke out a small anchor, tied it to a stout line on the ship, had a picked crew take the anchor out in a rowboat ahead of *Constitution* and drop the anchor into the sea. Then sailors manned the capstan bar on *Constitution* and pulled her up to the anchor. This process was known as "walking" a ship forward. When *Constitution* reached her anchor it was hauled up and the entire process repeated.

Walking a ship forward was not, however, a uniquely American idea. When the British saw what was happening, they too sent out kedges. The relative distance between the two forces remained the same. Then the British had an idea—they called out long boats from all the ships in their squadron, attached lines from the long boats to *Shannon* and had crews from seven warships pull the frigate along. This was a stunt Hull could not match. If evening and a slight breeze had not descended, *Constitution* would have been lost. But under the breeze, the graceful Humphreys frigate sprang forward, picking up her long boats as she went. The English could not do that—they had to stop and pick up their boat's crews. But, once again, the wind died.

All through the night and another windless day, *Constitution* labored fruitlessly to increase the distance between herself and the British ships. Then, as evening approached on the second day, storm clouds appeared. Hull immediately ordered all sails furled and the ship battened down as if a terrible tempest was approaching. The British captains, a mile or two behind him, saw his maneuver and repeated it. But as soon as the squall (that's all it was, as Hull well knew) hid *Constitution*, Hull ordered all sails set and, while the English frigates were still battening their hatches, *Constitution* sped away at 12 knots. By morning not a sail was to be seen on the horizon and Hull had won a race that was to become legendary among seafaring men through the years.

"Her sides are made of iron!"

But winning a race was not exactly the kind of victory Mr. Madison had had in mind when he permitted the frigates to put to sea. As far as Washington could see, the U.S. navy had accomplished nothing except escape from superior force. Madison sent orders that U.S. frigates were to stay in harbor once they returned.

Hull knew very well about this order. But, when he sailed *Constitution* into Boston, he had not actually received it. Borrowing money from a friend, he took on supplies as quickly as possible and then sailed on August 2, before the hateful instructions arrived. For this, as he realized, he could easily be court-martialed. Not only did he set sail from Boston, but he headed straight into the lion's jaws at Halifax, Nova Scotia, again looking for trouble. This time he found what he wanted—a single British frigate of *Constitution*'s class. On the afternoon of August 19, 1812, the sails and spars of H.M.S. *Guerriere*, 38, hove into view. The English frigate shortened sail and confidently awaited the Americans.

Confidently? Yes, because during fourteen years of war against the French no single British ship had ever yielded to anything like equal force. Because the U.S. navy was regarded as a kind of undisciplined privateering service, and referred to by *The Times* of London as "bastards and outlaws" sailing "green fir-built frigates," which, when inevitably captured, would prove worthless to His Majesty's navy.

Guerriere was originally a French frigate. She had been captured by the British and taken into the royal navy. Her captain was James Richard Dacres, an able mariner who entertained nothing but contempt for American frigates. Dacres had expressed this contempt by sending a note to Commodore Rodgers on the outbreak of war, inviting him to set to sea as Captain Dacres "would be happy to meet him or any other frigate of equal force to *President*, off Sandy Hook [New Jersey], for the purpose of having a few moments tête-à-tête."

Hull knew nothing of Dacres' invitation. He did know that he'd been drilling his men at the guns daily in the best Truxtun-Preble tradition, that they were not exactly "bastards" and "oulaws," but rather Maryland and New England sailor-men who had a personal bone to pick with His Majesty's navy over this impressment business. He also knew

July 1812: Constitution *is towed into Boston harbor.*

he commanded one of the finest frigates in the world, if not *the* finest.

Captain Dacres was eager to open the action. As *Constitution* bore down on him, he opened fire. *Guerriere*'s cannon roared rapidly but inaccurately, the shot falling short. For forty-five minutes *Constitution* advanced on *Guerriere*, her guns silent. Now some of the British cannonballs were beginning to strike. One of them bounced off *Constitution*'s hull and caused a gunner to cry out, "Hurrah, boys, her sides are made of iron!" Which remark gave birth to the nickname that was to stick to *Constitution* forever after—"Old Ironsides." Closer now, and closer, and while it fairly rained British cannonballs, Hull held his fire.

Lieutenant Richard Morris asked Hull if he could give the order to open fire.

"Not yet, Lieutenant, not yet," the old man replied grimly.

Closer and yet closer. Now the Americans could actually see the British gunners serving their cannon through *Guerriere*'s gun ports.

"No, Mr. Morris—not yet, not yet," Hull insisted.

Then, when the two frigates were much less than a pistol shot apart, Captain Isaac Hull leaped into the air (splitting his pants open as he did so) and screamed, "Now, boys! Pour it into them!"

Constitution let loose a terrible broadside that enveloped *Guerriere* like a storm cloud. Again and again *Constitution*'s broadside poured forth. Within fifteen minutes *Guerriere* lost her mizzenmast, sprung her mainmast and was hulled so badly that water poured into her faster than it could be pumped out. Seeing their enemy's plight, the American gunners shouted to each other, "Hull her, boys, hull her!"

Like a deer, *Constitution* then sprang ahead of her enemy

and sailed slowly across her bows. While she did so she poured a fearful raking broadside into the British ship, cannonballs sweeping lengthwise through *Guerriere*, dismounting guns, killing crews and knocking down her remaining masts. *Guerriere* was now a helpless hulk rolling in the sea. When, with the ships almost touching, Captain Dacres called for boarders to take *Constitution* by hand-to-hand fighting, before the British crew could muster, American marines in *Constitution*'s topmasts cut them down with deadly accurate rifle fire from their Kentucky "long guns."

With *Guerriere* a smoking wreck, Hull sailed off a short distance to repair damage aboard *Constitution*. This proved to be slight. And when *Constitution* sailed back down upon her hapless foe at sunset, Captain Dacres surrendered. The royal navy ensign came down for the first time in more than ten years.

Aboard *Guerriere* twenty-three had been killed, fifty-six more badly wounded. Aboard *Constitution* but fourteen men had become casualties. The British frigate was in such bad shape that during the night her people were transferred to *Constitution* and the wreck burned. Hull sailed back to Boston with his prisoners and with his captured English battle flag that would be spread at Dolley Madison's feet.

Constitution *towers over the wrecked* Guerriere.

4

"You Have No Right to Demand Anything!"

THE COUNTRY WENT WILD WITH REJOICING. NOT ONLY FOR *Constitution;* by the time she reached Boston with news of her victory, the nation was already celebrating the defeat of H.M.S. *Alert*, 20, by the American light frigate *Essex*, 32, and the destruction of H.M.S. *Frolic*, 20, by the American *Wasp*, 18. Three British battle flags—and more to come. For in October 1812 Stephen Decatur, commanding *United States*, 44 (affectionately known throughout the service as "Old Wagon"), came upon H.M.S. *Macedonian*, 38, and reduced her to a flaming wreck within two hours.

Congress voted thanks and, more important, prize money to all hands ($50,000 to *Constitution*, for example) for these

The Wasp *tangles with the British sloop of war* Frolic.

triumphs. Cities such as Boston, New York and Philadelphia gave memorial banquets and swords and keys of the city to officers and crews. At a triumphal ball given by the President's lady in Washington, while Dolley Madison marveled at the assembled captured British battle flags, Navy Secretary Paul Hamilton cried out, "Never forget that it is to Captains Bainbridge and Stewart that you really owe these victories!" He might have included Preble, Truxtun and Humphreys, the men who'd made the new U.S. navy, pound for pound, the most formidable fighting service in the world. As for Captain William Bainbridge—at that very moment he was doing something he would have preferred over attendance at any ball.

The End of Java

When *Constitution* returned to Boston in August 1812, after beating *Guerriere*, Isaac Hull was transferred to head the navy yards at Boston. Another one of Preble's boys, William Bainbridge, the man who had accidentally lost *Philadelphia* in Tripoli harbor, took command. Bainbridge was a commodore however, and it seemed only right to the Navy Department that he be given a fleet to command. Therefore, besides *Constitution* he was charged with squadron command over *Essex*, 32, a light frigate, and *Hornet*, 18, a sloop of war. His orders were fairly general—make as much trouble as possible for the British, especially in the West Indies. So ordered, so done.

Although *Constitution* and *Hornet* were ready to sail from Boston, *Essex* was still fitting out at Philadelphia. Bainbridge was impatient. So he sailed anyway, having first sent off a letter to David Porter, captain of *Essex*, saying, "Leave at once for West Indies and intercept British merchantmen." Bainbridge added that he would get in touch with Porter later on by dropping off letters for him at certain seaports in the West Indies. The only trouble with this plan was that the United States had no consuls and few friends in the West Indies. Therefore Bainbridge hit upon the idea of addressing Porter as "Captain James Yeo, of the British battleship *Southampton*" and leaving the letters with resident British consuls in the islands. Bainbridge was willing to bet that none of them knew Yeo (who did exist) or had ever seen *Southampton* (which also existed). His gamble paid off; some of his letters were received by Porter, but Bainbridge was never to see *Essex* again. For after missing a rendezvous with

*Commodore
William Bainbridge*

Constitution in the south Atlantic, Porter took his light frigate through the Strait of Magellan and into the Pacific Ocean. There he cruised for one year, burning British merchantmen and destroying Great Britain's entire whaling industry before he was himself captured by superior forces.

Meanwhile, *Constitution* and *Hornet* prowled down into the West Indies. They found the British sloop of war *Bonne Citoyenne*, 18, laying in Bahia, Brazil, and she seemed such a perfect match for *Hornet* that Captain James Lawrence, commanding the American sloop, invited the British captain to step outside the neutral harbor and fight it out, promising that the *Constitution* would take no part in the battle. But the captain of *Bonne Citoyenne* had little faith in such promises and refused. So *Hornet* stayed at Bahia, blockading the Englishman while *Constitution* sailed off in search of bigger prey. On December 29, 1812, she found it in the form of H.M.S. *Java,* 38, off the coast of Brazil.

Captain Henry Lambert, commanding *Java,* had not heard of the fate of *Guerriere* or *Macedonian.* Even if he had he would never have refused battle. Although, like all British frigates of her class, *Java* mounted but 38 guns as opposed to *Constitution*'s 44, His Majesty's navy had never in history cared to make such contemptible calculations. Frigates such as *Java,* with captains such as Lambert (a heavy disciplinarian, known as a flogger) and stout English crews, had fought French or Dutch ships of more than 50 guns and won. Furthermore, at this moment *Java* was carrying a crew and a half since she was carrying a draft of English sailors to India, she was more heavily built than most ships of her class, and she was rated the fastest frigate in the royal navy. So when Lambert saw *Constitution* standing in toward him, he made sail directly for the American frigate.

Java closed in from windward, trying to cross *Constitution*'s bows for a rake. But Bainbridge's crew aloft spun *Constitution*'s yards so that she seemed to dance around in the water. The two frigates plowed ahead side by side, exchanging roaring broadsides. One of *Java*'s guns shot away *Constitution*'s wheel (driving a copper bolt into Bainbridge's thigh), but the big frigate was steered by ropes attached directly to the rudder stem below decks. Once again *Java* tried to come around in front of *Constitution* to rake her.

The effort failed and brought disaster. *Java* had already been so badly hit at the water line that she stalled in her maneuver and it was *Constitution* that circled her enemy, pouring in frightful raking broadsides front and rear. Aboard

The destruction of Java

the British ship the junior lieutenants were yelling and running around beating seamen over the head with the flat of their swords. Somehow they managed to bring *Java* around so that her bowsprit entangled *Constitution*'s port quarter. British buglers called for boarders to take the American ship in hand-to-hand fighting. But as Captain Lambert ran forward to lead the attack he was shot down by U.S. marines —only the first among many casualties exacted by the sharpshooters stationed in the American topmasts. When *Constitution* pulled clear of *Java*, she jerked off the English frigate's bowsprit, and her foremast quickly followed.

For another quarter of an hour the two ships ran side by side exchanging broadsides. By now everything aboard *Java* was a shambles. Her crew was half wounded, her guns firing raggedly, and now her mizzenmast came down. Bainbridge pulled away for a while to straighten up his decks and then came sailing back. Just at that moment *Java*'s mainmast pitched over, and the surviving officers (Lambert was dead) surrendered the vessel. *Java* had suffered 48 killed and 150 wounded against *Constitution*'s 24 casualties. Furthermore, the English frigate was such a wreck that Bainbridge ordered her burned on the spot, taking the English crew with him as prisoners back to Bahia, where they were released on parole (their word not to fight again against the United States). Then he sailed home to Boston, arriving early in January 1813.

Once again Bostonians cheered themselves hoarse, bells were rung, dinners given, balls held, Congress voted praise and prize money. Perhaps of more importance, opinion in England began to suffer a change. "Good God, can such things be?" demanded *The Times* of London—the same newspaper that had referred to bastards and outlaws and fir-built frigates. My Lords of the Admiralty began to snivel about the American frigates being really "disguised battle-ships." Stronger than English frigates they certainly were (though not so much stronger as their lopsided victories seemed to indicate), but line-of-battleships carried about 100 guns on three decks, not 44 guns on one deck—as the admiralty well knew. The defeat of *Java* caused the English sea lords to change their tactics. From thenceforth, English frigates would sail in pairs, their only chance against being ground up by the heavy American ships. And, in any event, the war against France being all but won, the admiralty was now prepared to throw hundreds of ships against the United States and impose a strict blockade.

Sir John Warren's Nightmare

The blockade was indeed strict. The American frigates and sloops found themselves caught in port, their harbors sealed by British squadrons so powerful they could not hope to fight their way out. And there was a depressing piece of news to go with this grim fact. *Constitution*, it will be recalled, had left *Hornet* blockading a British sloop in Bahia. Shortly afterward a British battleship appeared off that Brazilian harbor and chased *Hornet* away. Captain James Lawrence (another of Preble's boys) sailed north and fell in with H.M.S. *Peacock*, 18, in the West Indies. *Hornet* made quick work of the British sloop, sinking her in twenty minutes.

All to the good? Yes. But for this victory Lawrence was promoted to the command of *Chesapeake*, 38, then fitting out at Boston. Her officers and crew were new, but when H.M.S. *Shannon*, 38, commanded by Philip Broke, appeared off the harbor, Lawrence sallied forth at once. In the resulting battle *Chesapeake* was fairly beaten, and Lawrence himself killed (crying out "Don't give up the ship!" as he was carried below). The fact that this victory has ever since been considered one of the finest in British sea annals and that Captain Broke was made a baronet for it, indicates how much respect the admiralty had learned to feel for the U.S. navy. But it was an American defeat, and, combined with the tight British blockade, it seemed to spell the end of American resistance at sea.

The struggle between the crews of Chesapeake *and* Shannon

The year 1813, the year of the sea blockade, saw several interesting developments, however. One of these was Oliver Hazard Perry's naval triumph on Lake Erie ("We have met the enemy, and they are ours"), another was a dramatic increase in American privateering.

The Yankee privateers of the War of 1812 were something new at sea. No longer were they warmed-over merchant ships. Now they were built to do their job. And they were designed as Baltimore clippers, probably the best sailing-ship design in history. They were incredibly fast, heavily armed and crewed now by men who not only were anxious to strike back at the navy that had impressed them, but had often been trained on the American frigates and sloops of war.

For examples: the privateer *Yankee* of Providence took seven ships off Ireland; *Scourge* of New York and *Rattlesnake* of Philadelphia cruised the North Sea and ruined England's Baltic trade for 1813. *America* of Salem cruised right off England's Land's End, taking every ship, including the royal mail boats that came within sight. *Rambler* of Boston sailed to China and cut off English trade with the Far East; *Harpy* of Baltimore stopped all communication between Liverpool and Dublin for weeks.

Worse than that, when the admiralty sent out ships to sink or capture these impudent privateers, they ran into unpleasant surprises. For instance, H.M.S. *Dominica*, 14, succeeded in catching up with the privateer *Decatur*—only to be captured by a swarm of Yankee seamen sweeping over her decks. A big British frigate caught the privateer *Prince de Neufchatel* in a calm off Nantucket. Since neither ship could sail on a windless day, the Britisher put over several long boats loaded with hundreds of sailors and marines. But so fiercely did *Prince de Neufchatel*'s crew of thirty-seven fight, that after losing a hundred men (and the privateer too, which sailed away on the first breeze) the British frigate had to put back to Halifax for a new crew, while three privateers she had been watching put to sea.

In less than three years of the War of 1812, American privateers took over 1,344 English ships. They tore English commerce to pieces all over the world. The English governor of Jamaica declared that his island was under a state of siege from Yankee privateers. And when Admiral Sir John Warren, in command of the royal navy's North American station, sailed to the West Indies in a frigate to look into the matter, the trip turned into a nightmare. Not an hour of the day passed when he didn't sight the topsails of some American privateer. If he chased her she vanished—to go elsewhere to do harm. Elsewhere might be the English Channel itself. So badly were English shippers and merchants hurt that they gathered to petition Parliament to make peace with "that Power whose maritime strength we have impolitically held in contempt."

"*. . . before two suns have set you will be in action with the enemy.*"

It was almost an insoluble problem. If British frigates and sloops scattered to catch privateers, they could not blockade American ports. And that meant that American naval vessels would slip out into the Atlantic and do far more damage than any dozen privateers. For example, in March 1814 Captain Lewis Warrington dodged the British blockade of New York to take *Peacock*, 20, to sea. On April 27 he ran down the

British sloop *Epervier*, 18, which *Peacock* chewed up in fifteen minutes. After sending the English ship home as a prize, Warrington sailed to the English Channel to ruin British commerce. There he was joined by U.S.S. *Wasp*, 20, and now My Lords of the Admiralty fretted while the two ships took twenty prizes and declared Great Britain blockaded. When *Wasp* ran into H.M.S. *Reindeer*, 18, she captured it in a bloody battle that lasted an hour; when *Wasp* ran into H.M.S. *Avon*, 20, she sank her handily.

Something was obviously wrong with the entire British system of naval warfare. Sending out heavy brigs or sloops of 18 or 20 guns to deal with privateers, which might attack convoys, was no longer sufficient. The privateers were now able to chew up the cruisers. His Majesty's ships were simply, pound for pound, no match for the Americans. Thus when H.M.S. *Penguin*, 18, sailed into the south Atlantic looking for privateers, she met instead U.S.S. *Hornet*, 18, and was shot to pieces in fifteen minutes. What was wrong, as My Lords of the Admiralty later ruefully admitted, was that the American ships were better designed and built. Furthermore their crews were trained to shoot, which British crews rarely were. The American ships were, as Humphreys had intended decades before, "an overmatch for those of the enemy."

How much of an overmatch was finally and conclusively demonstrated when, in January 1815, *Constitution* again sailed into the Atlantic. She took advantage of a gale to slip out of Boston and past three British blockading frigates as if they were not there. Her captain was now Charles Stewart, the man who with Bainbridge had appealed to Madison to let the navy fight. His crew were picked men—everyone wanted to sail aboard "Old Ironsides," and Stewart declared that his men could sail and fight the ship without any officers at all.

The big frigate ran down the coast of France and Spain, burning British merchantmen as she went. Then she turned to the mid-Atlantic islands. But burning British merchant ships was dull work. In February the lieutenants sent a delegation to Stewart saying that the men begged to be taken into action against the royal navy. Stewart was another of Preble's boys and was, no doubt, a remarkable fighting officer. But his reply was clairvoyant—and even Preble's boys never claimed supernatural powers. What he said was, "Be content. I promise you that before two suns have set you will be in action with the enemy and it will not be with a single ship." How did he know? No one ever figured it out. But sure enough, as sun set two days later, on February 20, 1815, *Constitution* came upon two British warships. They were H.M.S. *Cyane*, 32, and H.M.S. *Levant*, 20.

Both the British ships were lighter than *Constitution*, but they had, between them, 52 guns. Maneuvering separately they could also rake *Constitution* fore and aft. A full moon arose as the firing began, and through the smoke Stewart could see *Cyane* bearing down to get astern of him for a rake. Quickly the *Constitution*'s topmast men spun the frigate's yards. She backed down hard and, before *Cyane* could get into position, had delivered a crushing raking broadside of her own into the British ship's bow. But ahead *Levant* was now approaching to rake *Constitution* from in front. Once again the topsail men sprang into action. The big frigate bounded forward and raked *Levant* frightfully. Once again *Cyane* bore down upon *Constitution*, and once again the American frigate spun handily around, this time absolutely crushing her enemy with a broadside. *Cyane*'s flag came fluttering down in surrender. Stewart sent a prize crew to take over *Cyane* and then ran down *Levant*, which surrendered by nine o'clock that night.

Constitution *capturing* Cyane *and* Levant

The news that reached London was that not only had *Constitution* broken through the blockade and burned out English commerce in the Bay of Biscay, but she had also captured two ships sent out to fight her. It was the final blow. In fact, when *Constitution* returned to Boston it was to learn that the war was over. Peace had been signed at Ghent, Belgium, on December 24, 1814. When the British newspapers learned that the peace included no concessions whatsoever from the United States, nor one inch of territory, they were highly indignant. Was it not true that they had burned Washington, D.C.? Had they not beaten the Americans on land in Canada and the Northwest? True, the Yankees had won another lake naval battle when Macdonough defeated a British fleet on Lake Champlain—but that, again, had been a defensive victory.

His Majesty's government, however, was well aware that the Americans had won nearly all the fights at sea and that Yankee privateers would soon put an end to the British merchant marine if not stopped. They knew too that not only more of the incomparable frigates but also line-of-battleships were now being rushed to completion in navy yards at Boston, Philadelphia, New York and Charleston. So although no one yet knew that Andrew Jackson and his Kentucky riflemen had absolutely destroyed the British invasion army at New Orleans, His Majesty's peace commissioners accepted the Duke of Wellington's advice. That grizzled old hero of the Napoleonic Wars, when asked what should be demanded of the Yankees as the price for peace replied, "Why you have no right to demand anything!"

And so it was. Nothing was changed by the war. But one thing changed—never again would American commerce or sailors be molested on the high seas. And never again would

September 11, 1814: Macdonough's victory on Lake Champlain

Great Britain lightly undertake to fight a nation that could put such a navy on the ocean. That became very important during the Civil War and even afterward when British-American relations grew strained. As one of the American peace commissioners remarked after the English and Americans sat down together to talk peace in Belgium, "It was a scene to be remembered. God grant that there may be always peace between the two nations." To that My Lords of the Admiralty could only say "Amen!"

5

The
"Tattered Ensign"

LUCK? HER NAME? WHY SHOULD CONSTITUTION HAVE WON a more cherished place in the hearts of her countrymen than *Constellation* or *United States*? The colloquial name "Old Ironsides" may have helped, and of course her record was perfect—never a defeat. Whatever it was, the big frigate was going to be as immortal as human skill could make her.

For sixteen years after the War of 1812, *Constitution* cruised the seas and oceans of the world as part of the United States navy. Her very first postwar cruise would especially have pleased Commodore Preble. It was a friendly visit to the port of Algiers in company with two other frigates, the whole squadron being commanded by Stephen Decatur. It

*Commodore
Stephen Decatur*

seemed that while the U.S. navy was fighting the British during the late war, the Bey of Algiers had seen fit to capture an American merchantman and enslave her crew. Decatur captured the Algerian flagship off Gibraltar and burned her, then cruised into Algiers harbor, decks cleared for action, with a new and novel proposal for the Bey. He suggested that the Bey release the Americans, sign a new peace treaty and —unheard of demand—asked that instead of receiving ransom for his slaves, the Bey pay an indemnity for them! The Bey agreed. And when Decatur moved on to visit Tunis and Tripoli with his squadron, the rulers of those pirates' nests also came up with indemnities. To make sure they didn't change their mind, Captain William Bainbridge followed Decatur's squadron with another, consisting of a new battleship, three heavy frigates and a gaggle of those deadly Baltimore schooners. That punctured the myth of Barbary usefulness for Britain. If even an upstart power like the United States could cow the pirates, then the pirates were of no further use in whittling down rival merchant marines. The

English and Dutch sent a huge fleet to Algiers in 1817 which ground that city to dust and put an end forever to Mediterranean piracy.

Nevertheless, the United States continued to maintain a squadron in the Mediterranean, and *Constitution* was often part of it. The year-long cruise was a prized assignment. Port leave in cities like Marseilles, Naples, Syracuse, Car-

Decatur collecting indemnity from the Bey of Algiers

tagena, Barcelona was exciting. One of the sailors' songs of
the period reflects the atmosphere of these Mediterranean
cruises:

> *I lost my hat in Cape de Gat,*
> *And where do you think I found it?*
> *Behind a stone at Port Mahon,*
> *With three pretty girls around it.*

So the famous frigate sailed down the years—until 1830.
That year the Navy Department decided that, what with the
new-fangled steamships coming along, *Constitution* would
soon be outclassed. Many of her timbers were rotten and
the cost of overhauling her would be more than she was
worth. It was decided to scrap her and bids were sought
from shipwreckers. But the Navy Department reckoned
without one Oliver Wendell Holmes, a young law student
in Boston. When Holmes heard of the plan to scrap *Constitution* he dashed off an angry poem to his local newspaper,
the *Boston Transcript*. The poem was printed on September
16, 1830, and it went like this:

> *Ay, tear the tattered ensign down!*
> *Long has it waved on high,*
> *And many an eye has danced to see*
> *That banner in the sky;*
> *Beneath it rang the battle-shout,*
> *And burst the cannon's roar:*
> *The meteor of the ocean air*
> *Shall sweep the clouds no more!*

> *Her deck, once red with heroes' blood,*
> *Where knelt the vanquished foe,*

When winds were hurrying o'er the flood
And waves were white below,
No more shall feel the victor's tread,
Or know the conquered knee:
The harpies of the shore shall pluck
The eagle of the sea!

O, better that her shattered hulk
Should sink beneath the wave!
Her thunders shook the mighty deep,
And there should be her grave:
Nail to the mast her holy flag,
Set every threadbare sail,
And give her to the god of storms,
The lightning and the gale!

Maybe poetry meant more to people in 1830; in any event protests from all over the country descended upon the Navy Department. Generations of American youngsters were going to be condemned to recite "Old Ironsides" in school graduation ceremonies, and, like the Barbary pirates, the Navy Department gave in to the old frigate's fame. She was towed up to Boston (old Captain Isaac Hull taking proud command as she entered the harbor) and there rebuilt. Her old timbers were taken out and replaced, her rigging respliced and a new suit of sails provided while new guns and ammunition hoists were built into her. Then she was recommissioned.

Constitution continued to sail as part of the fighting navy until 1855. She cruised yearly to Europe and once around the world, used mainly as a training ship for naval cadets. During the Civil War she was moved from her berth at Annapolis to Newport to save her from Confederate raiding

parties, and after the war she continued her naval-training career. She was again rebuilt in 1870 (while under the command of a Lieutenant Commander George Dewey, who would one day sink a Spanish fleet in Manila Bay) and represented the United States navy at the great Paris Exposition of 1877. But after that her fame seemed eclipsed. By 1900 few people knew that the old hulk, slowly rotting in Boston harbor (with a wooden shed built over her decks), was the once mighty *Constitution*. But under the wave of patriotic frenzy that accompanied the Spanish-American War, the old frigate was found and her condition proclaimed a national disgrace.

During 1906–1907, *Constitution* was once again rebuilt, the shed removed from her decks and her masts restored. She became a naval museum and she was again rebuilt in 1927! This last time the money was raised from schoolchildren's penny contributions. And in 1927, *Constitution* was not simply rebuilt in the sense of having her old timbers replaced. This time she was rebuilt according to the original Humphreys design with a store of wood the Navy Department had been keeping since 1856. Entirely new masts and spars were raised and it was not until March 1930 that the work was done. Then the big frigate embarked on a career of exhibition cruises and visits to American cities from Maine to Oregon, sailed by a specially trained crew of forty-two men. At her mast she flew the original Star-Spangled Banner, the fifteen-starred flag she had borne in battle. Probably very few of the thousands who visited her in every port fully appreciated the trim Humphreys lines and the daring sweep of those high masts, or the remarkable power of those long 24-pounder cannon that poked through her gun ports. And perhaps they knew but little of the details of her history. It didn't matter. "Old Ironsides" had by now become a national symbol and a national monument, as important in the American myth as Bunker Hill or the Alamo or the battlefield at Gettysburg. It was certain now that she would never ever be scrapped but would, if necessary, be rebuilt over the years again and again.

She is there today, in drydock at Boston harbor, open to the public most days. You can go aboard and wonder at her great timbers, admire the agility of those old sailors who scrambled up her rigging in any kind of weather, pat the shining barrels of the long 24s, take a look at all sorts of old-time sailing gear and portraits of her famous commanders, from Silas Talbot and Isaac Hull and Edward Preble to Admiral Ernest King, Chief of Naval Operations, who made *Constitution* his flagship during World War II. She is more than 170 years old now—and still the pride of the United States navy.

Chronology

1794. Congress votes to build six frigates, designed by Joshua Humphreys.

SEPTEMBER 20, 1797. The frigate *Constitution*, 44, is launched in Boston harbor.

JULY 4, 1798. *Constitution* sets out on her first cruise, under Captain Samuel Nicholson.

1798–1799. *Constitution* cruises the Caribbean against French privateers under Captain Silas Talbot.

1803–1804. *Constitution* blockades Tripoli and bombards harbor under Captain Edward Preble.

1806. *Constitution* overawes the Bey of Tunis, under Captain John Rodgers.

JULY, 1812. *Constitution* escapes a British squadron, under Captain Isaac Hull.

AUGUST 19, 1812. *Constitution*, under Captain Isaac Hull, defeats *Guerriere*.

DECEMBER 29, 1812. *Constitution*, under Captain William Bainbridge, defeats *Java*.

JANUARY, 1815. *Constitution* chews up British commerce off France and Spain, under Captain Charles Stewart.

FEBRUARY 20, 1815. *Constitution*, under Captain Stewart, defeats *Cyane* and *Levant*.

1815–1816. *Constitution*, under Captain Stephen Decatur, frightens the Barbary pirates into submission.

1817–1830. *Constitution* cruises the world on peaceful missions.

1830. *Constitution* is condemned to be scrapped, but is saved by Oliver Wendell Holmes and his poem "Old Ironsides."

1830–1831. *Constitution* is rebuilt.

1855. *Constitution* becomes a training ship.

1870. *Constitution*, under Captain George Dewey, is rebuilt again.

1877. *Constitution* represents the U.S. navy at the Paris Exhibition.

1906–1907. *Constitution* rebuilt again.

1927. *Constitution* rebuilt yet again and sailed on cruises to U.S. ports.

TODAY. *Constitution* a naval museum in drydock at Boston harbor.

For Further Reading

FORESTER, C. S. *The Age of Fighting Sail: The Story of the Naval War of 1812.* New York: Doubleday & Co., 1956.

HANSEN, HARRY. *Old Ironsides: The Fighting* Constitution. New York: Random House, Inc., 1955.

HOLLIS, IRA N. *The Frigate* Constitution: *The Central Figure of the Navy Under Sail.* Boston: Houghton Mifflin Co., 1931.

HORSMAN, REGINALD. *Causes of the War of 1812.* New York: A. S. Barnes & Co., Inc., 1939.

MAHAN, CAPTAIN ALFRED T. *Sea Power in Its Relations to the War of 1812.* Boston: Little, Brown & Co., 1905.

MERCIER, HENRY J. *Life in a Man-of-War, or, Scenes in "Old Ironsides" During Her Cruise in the Pacific, by a Fore-top-man with Preface by Elliot Snow.* Boston: Houghton Mifflin Co., 1927.

PERKINS, BRADFORD. *Prologue to War: England and the United States, 1805–1812.* Berkeley: University of California Press, 1961.

PRATT, FLETCHER. *The Compact History of the United States Navy.* New York: Hawthorn Books, Inc., 1957.

Index